Every Kid's Guide to
Making Friends

Written by
JOY BERRY

CHILDRENS PRESS ®
CHICAGO

About the Author and Publisher

Joy Berry's mission in life is to help families cope with everyday problems and to help children become competent, responsible, happy individuals. To achieve her goal, she has written over two hundred self-help books for children from birth through age twelve. Her work revolutionized children's publishing by providing families with practical, how-to, living skills information that was previously unavailable in children's books.

Joy gathered a dedicated team of experts, including psychologists, educators, child developmentalists, writers, editors, designers, and artists, to form her publishing company and to help produce her work.

The company, Living Skills Press, produces thoroughly researched books and audio-visual materials that successfully combine humor and education to teach subjects ranging from how to clean a bedroom to how to resolve problems and get along with other people.

Managing Editor: Ellen Klarberg
Copy Editor: Kate Dickey
Contributing Editors: Libby Byers, Nancy Cochran, Maureen Dryden, Yona Flemming, Kathleen Mohr, Susan Motycka
Editorial Assistant: Sandy Passarino

Art Director: Laurie Westdahl
Design: Abigail Johnston, Laurie Westdahl
Production: Abigail Johnston, Caroline Rennard
Illustrations designed by: Bartholomew
Inker: Tuan Pham
Colorer: Tuan Pham
Composition: Curt Chelin

Friends are a very important part of your life.

In **EVERY KID'S GUIDE TO MAKING FRIENDS,** you will learn the following:
- what a friend is,
- what guidelines to follow for making friends,
- what guidelines to follow for keeping friends, and
- that friends are important.

A friend is someone you like.

A friend is also someone who likes you.

There are different kinds of friends.
One kind of friend is called an *acquaintance.*
Acquaintances spend very little time together.
They might like each other, but they do not know
each other very well.

Most people have many acquaintances.

Another kind of friend is called a *playmate*.
Playmates see each other often.
They enjoy playing and doing things together.

Most people have several playmates.

Another kind of friend is called a **best friend.**
Best friends have very special feelings for each other.
Best friends

- love,
- respect, and
- trust each other.

Best friends spend as much time together as they can.
They share their

- thoughts,
- feelings,
- experiences, and
- possessions.

Best friends require time and energy, so having too many best friends at one time can be difficult.

Most people have one or two best friends at a time.

If you are like most people, you need to have friendships that include

- acquaintances,
- playmates, and
- best friends.

If you are like most people, you will have at one time
- many acquaintances,
- several playmates, and
- one or two best friends.

It will be easier to develop friendships if you follow these six guidelines to making friends:

Guideline 1. Show an interest in the other person.

Think about what you would like to know about the person.

Find out about these things by asking the other person questions.

If the person does not want to answer your questions, respect his or her privacy and talk about something else.

Guideline 2. Use the other person's name.

Remember that a person's name is very important. Most people like to hear their names used.

Call the other person by name as often as you can. Do not use someone's nickname unless the person wants you to.

Guideline 3. Talk about subjects that will interest the other person.

Find out what the person enjoys talking or learning about. Talk about those subjects.

Talk about something else if the person is not interested in what you are saying.

Guideline 4. Listen to the other person.

When the other person is talking
- look at him or her and
- do not interrupt.

Encourage the other person to talk by asking
questions.
Then listen carefully to what the person is saying.

Guideline 5. Help the other person feel important.

Remember that every person makes a special contribution to the world. What each person gives cannot be contributed by anyone else.

Talk with the other person about his or her special contribution.

Help the person realize it makes him or her very important.

Guideline 6. Help the other person feel special.

Think about the things that make the person different from anyone else.

Tell the other person about his or her special qualities.

Encourage the person to appreciate and enjoy them.

Once you have created a friendship, it is important for you to do your best to keep it.
It will be easier to keep friendships if you follow these eight guidelines to keeping friends:

Guideline 1. Accept the other person as is.

Do not try to force the other person to change or be different from the way he or she is.

Guideline 2. Appreciate the other person.

Think good thoughts about the person.

Share your good thoughts about the person with him or her.

Praise the person whenever you can.

Guideline 3. Encourage the other person.

Tell the person that he or she is doing OK.

Give the person courage, hope, and confidence to keep trying.

Guideline 4. Empathize with the other person.

Try to put yourself in the other person's place.

Try to understand how the other person thinks and feels.

Respect his or her thoughts and feelings.

Guideline 5. Do not nag and argue with the other person.

Remember that nagging and arguing can create a bad situation.

Try to resolve problems and disagreements by talking in a kind way. Do not
- scream and yell,
- say mean things, and
- talk about old problems that have already been resolved.

Guideline 6. Apologize to the other person whenever necessary.

It is important to tell the people who will be affected by your actions about your mistakes or wrongdoings.

If what you have done has hurt the other person,
- admit it,
- say you are sorry,
- ask the person to forgive you, and
- do your best to make things right again.

Guideline 7. Forgive the other person whenever necessary.

Do whatever you can to make the person feel better when he or she makes a mistake or does something wrong.

Forgive the other person.

Then do your best to forget the incident.

Guideline 8. Do something special for the other person.

Do something that will make the person happy.

You can
- do favors,
- make special treats, or
- give the person small gifts.

Friends don't just happen.
It takes work to create a friendship.

However, the good things you do to make friends will be worthwhile because friends make life more interesting. Friends can also bring you joy and happiness.

Friends can comfort you when you are feeling sad.

Friends can also help you when you are in trouble.

You can make friends by being the kind of friend you want to have.